Deep Fryer Reci

An Updated Cookbook of Tasty, Fried Dish Ideas!

BY

Julia Chiles

Copyright 2020 - Julia Chiles

License Notes

No part of this Book can be reproduced in any form or by any means including print, electronic, scanning or photocopying unless prior permission is granted by the author.

All ideas, suggestions and guidelines mentioned here are written for informative purposes. While the author has taken every possible step to ensure accuracy, all readers are advised to follow information at their own risk. The author cannot be held responsible for personal and/or commercial damages in case of misinterpreting and misunderstanding any part of this Book

Table of Contents

Introduction 6

Start your morning with a deep fryer breakfast recipe. It'll fill you up for your day ahead… 8

   1 – Deep Fryer Sausage & Cheese Breakfast Empanadas 9

   2 – Deep-Fried French Toast Breakfast 11

There are SO many kinds of lunch, dinner, side dish, and appetizer deep fryer recipes you can choose for a special meal or party. Here are some of the best… 13

   3 – Deep Fryer Beer Batter Fish 14

   4 – Deep Fried Calamari 16

   5 – Deep Fryer Cheese Bites 19

   6 – Deep Fried Potato Tots 21

   7 – Deep Fryer Southern Chicken 23

   8 – Deep Fried Falafel with Feta Cheese 26

   9 – Deep Fryer Chimichangas 29

   10 – Deep Fried Onion Rings 32

   11 – Deep Fryer Okra 35

   12 – Deep Fried Zucchini Fritters 37

13 – Deep Fryer Corn Dogs 40

14 – Deep Fried Green Tomatoes 42

15 – Deep Fryer Corn Fritters 45

16 – Deep Fried Sweet Potato Latkes 47

17 – Deep Fryer Spring Rolls 50

18 – Deep Fried Perfect Fries 53

19 – Deep Fryer Lime Chili Chicken Wings 55

20 – Deep Fried Cauliflower 57

21 – Deep Fryer Jalapeno Poppers 60

22 – Deep Fried Pork Chops 63

23 – Deep Fryer Sweet Potato Chicken Bites 66

24 – Deep Fried Chicken Livers 68

25 – Deep Fryer Mac Cheese Nuggets 70

Deep frying gives desserts a new look and a new taste. Try some of these favorites soon… 73

26 – Deep Fried Blueberry Sugar Egg Rolls 74

27 – Deep Fryer Churros 76

28 – Deep-Fried Cookie Dough, Oreo® Twinkie® Balls 79

29 – Deep Fryer Apple Fritters 81

30 – Deep Fried Funnel Cakes 83

Conclusion 85

Author's Afterthoughts 86

Introduction

What would you think if I told you about a wonderful method of cooking that makes meals and snacks unique from any other? Deep-frying is that method.

How can you create tasty dishes that utilize deep-frying?

Check out the recipes in this fabulous deep fryer cookbook.

Can snacks and appetizers be deep-fried, in addition to meals and desserts?

Yes! Although many deep-fried recipes are meals, I include innovative deep fryer recipes for snacks and appetizers, too.

You can find deep frying in many countries, and street food offered on every continent contains many choices that are deep-fried. There are many foods that can be made with a deep fryer, and it brings out a rich taste in everything cooked in it.

Some of the foods you can deep-fry include poultry, meat, vegetables, and fish. Onion rings, French fries, hush puppies, and doughnuts are quite popular when deep-fried. There are so many more though, from tempura in Japan to pizza, candy bars, and even peanut butter & jelly sandwiches!

Deep-fried treats like funnel cakes are perennial favorites at festivals and as street foods. The taste simply cannot be duplicated any other way. Turn the page, and read on…

Start your morning with a deep fryer breakfast recipe. It'll fill you up for your day ahead...

1 – Deep Fryer Sausage & Cheese Breakfast Empanadas

Here's a handy, savory breakfast that you can hold in one hand. That makes it perfect for breakfast on the go. These empanadas can be stuffed with all kinds of breakfast favorite ingredients, from sausage to bacon, cheese, eggs, and more.

Makes 8 Servings

Cooking + Prep Time: 55 minutes

Ingredients:

- 2 x 8-count containers of biscuits, refrigerated

Optional: 2 tbsp. of butter, unsalted

- 1 lb. of breakfast sausage, cooked
- 1/2 lb. cooked, crumbled bacon + extra if desired
- 1 cup of cheddar cheese shreds
- 1 cup of hash browns (frozen is fine)
- 4 to 6 eggs, large
- Salt, kosher, as desired
- Pepper, ground, as desired

To deep fry: oil, canola

Instructions:

1. In deep pan, add butter. Cook sausage. Toss in crumbled, cooked bacon. Mix well. Add hash browns.

2. Mix eggs in bowl and season as desired. Pour into pan.

3. Stir beaten eggs into meat till cooked as you desire. Top with cheese but don't stir it. Allow it to sit on top and melt a bit.

4. Roll out biscuits one after another. Place filling on them. Don't make them too full. Fold them over. Crimp edges well. Allow them to sit as you do the next ones.

5. Deep fry one empanada after another. Flip so they get puffy and golden evenly. Allow them to cool a little and serve warm.

2 – Deep-Fried French Toast Breakfast

If you love French toast, you'll love it even more when it's deep-fried! The outside is crispy, and the inside is soft, like the French toast that you have in restaurants. Syrup and powdered sugar make it complete.

Makes 4 Servings

Cooking + Prep Time: 25 minutes

Ingredients:

- 6 eggs, large
- 5 1/2 tsp. of sugar, granulated
- 1/4 tsp. of salt, kosher
- 2 cups of milk, whole
- 1 cup of flour, all-purpose

To deep fry: 2 quarts of oil, vegetable

- 8 x 1" thick slices of bread, French

Instructions:

1. Beat eggs, salt sugar together in medium bowl. Whisk in milk, then flour. Whisk till you have a smooth mixture.

2. Heat the oil in deep-fryer to 375F.

3. Soak slices of bread in egg mixture till egg penetrates through to middle of bread. Wipe off any excess egg. Fry in deep fryer a few slices at a time, so they don't become overcrowded. Cook till both sides are golden brown and not soggy in middle anymore, usually four minutes or so. Drain on plate lined with paper towels and serve.

There are SO many kinds of lunch, dinner, side dish, and appetizer deep fryer recipes you can choose for a special meal or party. Here are some of the best...

3 - Deep Fryer Beer Batter Fish

This is a classic beer batter, perfect for making deep fryer fish. It can also be used tastily for onion rings and calamari.

Makes 4 Servings

Cooking + Prep Time: 45 minutes

Ingredients:

- 1/2 cup of corn starch
- 1 1/2 tsp. of baking powder, reduced sodium
- 3/4 tsp. of salt, kosher
- 1/2 tsp. of seasoning, Creole
- 1/4 tsp. of paprika, sweet
- 1/4 tsp. of pepper, cayenne
- 1 cup of flour, all-purpose
- 1/2 cup of milk, 2%
- 1/3 cup of beer (nonalcoholic beer is fine, too)
- 2 cups of saltines, crushed
- 4 x 6-oz. fillets, cod

To deep-fry: oil, canola

Instructions:

1. In shallow bowl, combine corn starch, salt, baking powder, paprika, Creole seasoning, 1/2 cup of flour and cayenne pepper. Stir in beer and milk till you have a smooth texture.

2. Place remaining flour and crackers in separate bowls. Coat the fillets using flour. Dip in the batter and coat fillets with crushed crackers.

3. In deep fryer, heat the oil to 375F. Fry the fish in small batches for two to three minutes per side till golden brown in color. Drain with paper towels and serve.

4 - Deep Fried Calamari

When you marinate this calamari in light buttermilk, it lessens that rubber band texture some calamari attains when it's cooked. It's also helpful in creating a crisp, light batter, making the calamari more flavorful.

Makes Various # of Servings

Cooking + Prep Time: 1 hour 20 minutes + 1 hour marinating time

Ingredients:

- 1 1/2 lbs. of calamari, cleaned, bodies sliced in 1/2" rings, with whole tentacles
- 2 cups of buttermilk, shaken well
- 3 cups of flour, all-purpose
- 2 tbsp. of salt, kosher

To deep fry: oil, canola

- 1 8-wedge-cut lemon, fresh

Instructions:

1. Place the calamari in medium-sized non-reactive bowl. Then cover them with buttermilk. Marinate in refrigerator for one hour.

2. Heat oven to 200F. Place rack in center. Line cookie sheet with several paper towel layers.

3. Combine salt flour in large sized bowl. Whisk, aerating and breaking up lumps. Set bowl aside.

4. Pour two inches oil in deep fryer. Heat on high till it reaches 400F.

5. Remove handful of calamari from buttermilk. Place in flour mixture and coat evenly. Transfer the calamari to strainer. Shake excess flour gently back into bowl.

6. Place calamari carefully in oil. Fry till golden brown, one minute or so. Transfer to cookie sheet with paper towels. Season as desired. Place cookie sheet in oven and keep warm.

7. Return oil to 400F. Repeat frying process with the rest of the calamari, making five or six batches. Serve with wedges of fresh lemon.

5 – Deep Fryer Cheese Bites

Cheese cubes or curds dipped first in flour, then in beer, before frying, are appetizers that will tempt all your guests. Don't be surprised when they vanish quite swiftly.

Makes 12 Servings

Cooking + Prep Time: 45 minutes

Ingredients:

- 1 lb. of cheddar cheese, cubed
- 1 1/4 cups of flour, all-purpose
- 1 cup of beer or nonalcoholic beer

To deep fry: oil, canola

Instructions:

1. Place 1/4 cup of flour in large zipper top plastic bag. Add the cheese, several pieces at a time. Shake and coat well.

2. Heat oil to 375F in deep fryer. In large-sized bowl, whisk the beer and remainder of flour. Dip cheese bites, several at a time, in batter. Fry in deep fryer for two to three minutes per side, till golden brown. Drain them on the paper towels and serve.

6 – Deep Fried Potato Tots

Fried potatoes are favorites in so many places. Potato tots have a crunchy exterior with a fluffy, piping hot inside that people just can't pass up. They are especially well-loved with ketchup.

Makes about 40-45 tots

Cooking + Prep Time: 1 1/2 hour

Ingredients:

- 2 medium potatoes, scrubbed
- 1 tbsp. of flour, all-purpose
- 1 tsp. of salt, fine + additional if needed

To fry: 1 1/2 – 2 cups oil, canola

Instructions:

1. Heat oven to 450F. Place rack in center. Place potatoes in oven. Bake till they pierce easily using a knife. They should still have firm centers. This takes 35-40 minutes.

2. When the potatoes are cool enough to be handled, peel skin away and discard it. Shred potatoes with box grater. Transfer potatoes to large bowl. Season as desired and mix till combined well.

3. Measure out 1 tsp. of potato mixture. Roll into short cylinder of about 1 1/2" in length and 3/4" in width. Place on cookie sheet. Repeat with the rest of the potato mixture.

4. Line another cookie sheet using paper towels and set it aside. Add enough oil to large fry pan to reach 1/4" up sides. Set on med-high till hot, five minutes.

5. Fry tots 8-10 pieces at a time, without overcrowding. Turn them once till both sides are golden brown, two to three minutes each batch.

6. Transfer tots to cookie sheet on paper towels. Season as desired. Serve promptly with your favorite dipping sauces.

7 – Deep Fryer Southern Chicken

All fried chicken is not the same, by a long shot! This Southern version of deep-fried chicken will open your eyes and leave you wanting for more.

Makes 6 Servings

Cooking + Prep Time: 55 minutes + 8 hours refrigeration time

Ingredients:

- 3 cups of buttermilk, whole
- 3 tsp. of salt, kosher
- 1 tsp. of pepper, ground
- 1 x 3-4 lb. cut up fryer/broiler chicken

To deep fry: oil, vegetable

- 2 cups of flour, all-purpose
- 1 tsp. of paprika, sweet
- 1 tsp. of garlic powder
- 1 tsp. of onion powder

Instructions:

1. Whisk 2 cups of buttermilk with 1 tsp. of salt 1/8 tsp. of pepper in shallow bowl. Add the chicken. Turn, coating well. Cover and place in refrigerator overnight.

2. Heat the oil to 375F in deep fryer. Place remainder of buttermilk in separate shallow bowl. In yet another shallow bowl, whisk the flour, paprika, onion powder and garlic powder, along with remainder of salt pepper.

3. Place 1/2 of flour mixture in another shallow bowl. Drain the chicken and discard marinade. Pat the chicken dry and dip it in the flour mixture and coat each side. Shake off any excess. Dip chicken into buttermilk and drain off excess.

4. For second breading coat, dip chicken in remainder of flour mixture and pat so coating adheres well.

5. Fry the chicken, several pieces at once, for four to five minutes per side, till browned with juices running clear. Drain chicken on the paper towels and serve.

8 – Deep Fried Falafel with Feta Cheese

These are traditional falafel, deep-fried for a perfect texture and taste. Plus, inside, there is a surprise: a salty, creamy feta cheese cube. They are especially wonderful served with hummus or Tzatziki sauce.

Makes 15-20 falafel

Cooking + Prep Time: 50 minutes

Ingredients:

- 1 1/3 cup of chickpeas (garbanzo beans) – soak for 24 hours in cold water
- 2 cloves of garlic
- 1 cup of packed parsley leaves, flat-leaf
- 1 cup of packed leaves, mint
- 1/2 tsp. of cumin, ground
- 1 tsp. of baking powder, reduced sodium
- 2 tsp. of salt, kosher
- 1 tsp. of pepper, ground
- 3 1/2 oz. of 1/2"-cubed feta cheese

Optional: 1 tbsp. of lemon juice, fresh-squeezed

- 2-5 tbsp. of water, filtered

To deep fry: oil, canola

Instructions:

1. Add soaked, drained garbanzo beans to bowl of food processor with salt, pepper, baking powder, garlic, cumin, mint and parsley. Blend into smooth paste. Add 2 tbsp. water as needed to smooth out the mixture.

2. Flatten 1/4 of falafel mixture against palm of hand. Place one cube feta cheese in center. Wrap falafel mixture around cheese, fully enclosing it. Roll in ball. Place on cookie sheet lined with baking paper. Repeat with the rest of the falafel mixture. You should only have one layer of balls on cookie sheet.

3. Add oil to deep fryer to measure three inches from bottom. Place on med. heat till it reaches 375F. Adjust heat, maintaining steady temperature.

4. Deep fry batches of falafel till golden brown outside and cooked through, three to five minutes. Drain them on layers of paper towels. Continue to fry till you have cooked all falafel. Serve with hummus or tzatziki.

9 – Deep Fryer Chimichangas

Southern cooking meets the American Southwest in these deep-fried chimichangas. They are so tasty; you may want to double the recipe and freeze the extras to be eaten whenever you like.

Makes 12 Servings

Cooking + Prep Time: 45 minutes

Ingredients:

- 1 lb. of beef, ground
- 1 x 16-oz. can of beans, refried
- 1/2 cup of onion, chopped finely
- 3 x 8-oz. cans of tomato sauce, low sodium
- 2 tsp. of chili powder
- 1 tsp. of garlic, minced
- 1/2 tsp. of cumin, ground
- 12 x 10" warmed tortillas, flour
- 1 x 4-oz. can of green chilies, chopped
- 1 x 4-oz. can of jalapeno peppers, chopped

To deep fry: oil, canola

- 1 1/2 cups of cheddar cheese shreds

Instructions:

1. Cook beef on med. heat in large-sized skillet till not pink anymore. Drain well. Stir in onion, beans, 1/2 cup of tomato sauce, cumin, chili powder and garlic.

2. Spoon 1/3 cup beef mixture near middle of tortillas. Fold edges nearest the filling over and cover it. Fold in each side. Roll them up. Fasten them with toothpicks.

3. In large sized pan, combine remainder of tomato sauce, chilies and peppers. Heat fully through.

4. Heat an inch of oil to 375F in deep fryer. Fry chimichangas for 1 1/2 – 2 minutes per side, till browned nicely. Drain using paper towels. Sprinkle cheese on top. Serve along with sauce.

10 – Deep Fried Onion Rings

Onion rings will probably never be as popular as French fries, but they make a great side dish for hamburgers and hot dogs. These onion rings offer an ultra-crisp coating, and you'll love dipping them in your favorite sauces.

Makes 3 Servings

Cooking + Prep Time: 35 minutes

Ingredients:

- 2 eggs, large
- 3/4 cup of flour, all-purpose
- 1/2 cup of milk, whole
- 2 1/2 tsp. of salt, kosher, + extra to season
- 1 1/2 cups of breadcrumbs, fine, dry
- 1 medium onion, yellow, sliced in 1/4 – 1/2" thick rounds – separate in rings

To deep-fry: 2 quarts of oil, vegetable

Instructions:

1. Line large-sized cookie sheet using baking paper. Set aside two more sheets of baking paper.

2. Combine flour plus 1 tsp. kosher salt in shallow, wide dish and set it aside. Combine milk and eggs in separate shallow dish. Mix till eggs have broken up and then set dish aside.

3. Mix last 1 1/2 tsp. of kosher salt with breadcrumbs in another shallow, wide dish and set it aside.

4. Toss one onion ring in flour mixture till coated evenly, to bread. Shake off excess. Dip ring in egg mixture till coated well and allow excess to drain off. Then toss ring in breadcrumb mixture and press to adhere crumbs to ring. Set breaded ring on cookie sheet prepared above. Repeat with remainder of onion rings and place them in one layer on cookie sheet. They shouldn't be touching.

5. When you have filled cookie sheet, cover onion rings with new sheet of baking paper. Continue to bread and place onion rings on new baking paper sheet till full. Repeat using third sheet of baking paper till all rings have been breaded and set aside.

6. Place oil in deep fryer. Heat on med-high till it has reached 375F.

7. Work in batches of eight rings or so at once. Drop rings in heated oil. Fry till golden brown, 45 seconds or so. Transfer rings to wire rack. Season as desired. Repeat with remainder of rings. Serve promptly.

11 - Deep Fryer Okra

These okra will deep-fry up golden brown, and with a bit of green freshness shining through. They are crunchy and quite addictive. Kids like dipping them in good old ketchup.

Makes 2 Servings

Cooking + Prep Time: 35 minutes

Ingredients:

- 3 tbsp. of buttermilk, light
- 1 1/2 cups of sliced okra, frozen thawed or fresh
- 2 tbsp. of flour, all-purpose
- 2 tbsp. of corn meal
- 1/4 tsp. of salt, kosher
- 1/4 tsp. of seasoning blend, herb-garlic
- 1/8 tsp. of pepper, ground

To deep-fry: oil, canola

Optional: extra kosher salt ground pepper

Instructions:

1. Pat the okra dry using paper towels. Pour buttermilk into shallow, wide bowl.

2. In separate shallow bowl, combine corn meal, flour, seasoning blend, kosher salt ground pepper. Dip the okra in the buttermilk. Roll it in the corn meal mixture.

3. In deep fryer, heat 1" oil to 375F. Fry the okra, several pieces at once, for 1 1/2 – 2 1/2 minutes per side, till golden brown. Then drain them on the paper towels. Season as desired and serve.

12 – Deep Fried Zucchini Fritters

These tasty fritters puff up into many odd shapes when you deep fry them. They will disappear as quickly as you can finish frying them. They go especially well with Blue Cheese or Ranch dressing.

Makes 45-48 fritters

Cooking + Prep Time: 1 hour 10 minutes

Ingredients:

- 1 cup of flour, all-purpose
- 1 1/4 – 1 1/2 lbs. of unpeeled, grated zucchini
- 1 1/2 tsp. of baking powder, reduced sodium
- 2 tsp. of sugar, granulated
- 2 tsp. + 1 pinch salt, kosher
- 2 eggs, large
- 1/3 cup of milk, whole
- 1 tbsp. of melted butter, unsalted

To deep fry: oil, vegetable

- 1/3 cup of Parmesan cheese, grated

Instructions:

1. Spread zucchini on paper towels and allow to drain, 10 minutes or so.

2. Stir baking powder, flour, sugar 2 tsp. kosher salt together in large sized bowl.

3. Beat egg yolks thoroughly in separate bowl. Add and stir in melted butter and milk.

4. Beat egg whites with mixer set on med-high till they are foamy. Add pinch of kosher salt. Increase blender speed up to high. Beat till mixture forms still peaks.

5. Stir egg yolk mixture zucchini in flour mixture. Fold in egg whites carefully.

6. Pour 1-2" of oil in deep fryer. Heat to 375F.

7. Drop 1 tbsp. of batter at a time in hot oil. Don't crowd them. Fry and turn once till golden brown in color, three minutes or so. As they cook, transfer them to paper towels for draining. Continued to fry till you have used all the batter.

8. Shake fritters in paper bag with Parmesan cheese. Serve while hot.

13 – Deep Fryer Corn Dogs

Corn dogs are one of the highlights of festivals and fairs in the American Midwest. They're easy to deep-fry at home, too, so you can bring the good times back with you.

Makes 12 Servings

Cooking + Prep Time: 45 minutes

Ingredients:

- 1/2 cup of corn meal, yellow
- 1 cup of flour, all-purpose
- 1 tbsp. of sugar, granulated
- 3 tsp. of baking powder, reduced sodium
- 1 tsp. of salt, kosher
- 1/2 tsp. of mustard, ground
- 1/4 tsp. of paprika, sweet
- A dash of pepper, ground
- 1 beaten egg, large
- 1 cup of milk, evaporated

To deep fry: oil, vegetable

- 12 hot dogs
- 12 skewers

Instructions:

1. Whisk first eight ingredients in bowl. Whisk in milk and egg till barely blended. Then transfer to batter to tall glass.

2. Heat oil to 375F in deep fryer. Insert 12 skewers into 12 hot dogs. Dip the hot dogs in batter and let excess batter drip off.

3. Fry the corn dogs, several at once, for two to three minutes, till golden brown, while occasionally turning. Drain them on layered paper towels and serve promptly.

14 – Deep Fried Green Tomatoes

The main ingredients in this dish may be Southern, but the deep-frying is often done at supper clubs in New York state. They are wonderful, especially when you pair them with lemon slices and a bit of rémoulade.

Makes 4 Servings

Cooking + Prep Time: 1 hour 5 minutes

Ingredients:

- 1 egg, large
- 1/4 cup of milk, whole
- 2 cups of panko breadcrumbs
- 1 1/2 tsp. of lemon zest, packed loosely
- 2 tbsp. of tarragon, dried
- 1/4 cup of seasoning, Old Bay
- 4 cups of oil, vegetable
- 1 1/2 cups of flour, all-purpose
- 2 lbs. of sliced green tomatoes, heirloom

Instructions:

1. Place the milk and egg in medium-sized bowl. Whisk till combined well and set them aside. Place the lemon zest, breadcrumbs, Old Bay seasoning and tarragon in shallow, wide plate. Mix till combined evenly and set plate aside.

2. Heat the oil on med. heat in deep fryer or large-sized frying pan to 350F. Line plate using paper towels and set it aside.

3. Set up separate wide, shallow bowls with all-purpose flour, the egg wash and the breading.

4. Dry off tomato slices. Dip each in the flour. Shake off any excess. Dip them in the egg wash and allow the excess to drip off. Place in the breading dish. Firmly press to make sure the breading adheres well. Flip tomato slice and repeat. Then continue till you have breaded all the tomatoes.

5. Fry the sliced, breaded tomatoes till golden brown, about a minute per side. Drain them on plate lined with paper towels. Season and serve while they are still hot.

15 – Deep Fryer Corn Fritters

A single bite of these deep-fried fritters will take you back to the first time you had them. They're very popular, so you may want to double the recipe if you're having guests over. They are especially tasty with agave nectar or maple syrup.

Makes 32 fritters

Cooking + Prep Time: 35 minutes

Ingredients:

- 2 1/2 cups of flour, all-purpose
- 3 tsp. of baking powder, reduced sodium
- 2 tsp. of parsley flakes, dried
- 1 tsp. of salt, kosher
- 2 eggs, large
- 3/4 cup of milk, 2%
- 2 tbsp. of melted butter, unsalted
- 2 tsp. of onion, grated
- 1 x 15 1/4-oz. can of drained corn, whole kernel

To deep fry: oil, canola

Instructions:

1. Whisk the flour, parsley, salt baking powder in large sized bowl. In separate bowl, whisk milk, eggs, onion and butter till blended well. Add this to the dry ingredient mixture and stir till barely moistened. Add and fold in the corn.

2. Heat the oil to 375F in deep fryer. Drop the batter in tablespoonfuls, a few at a time, into the heated oil. Fry for two to three minutes per side, till golden brown, then drain them on layered paper towels. Serve.

16 – Deep Fried Sweet Potato Latkes

These savory-but-sweet potato latkes are a wonderful addition to your table for a dinner party or carry-in. This recipe allows them to glow with the spices of New Mexico.

Makes 4-6 Servings

Cooking + Prep Time: 1 hour 40 minutes

Ingredients:

For sour cream lime sauce

- 1 cup sour cream, light
- 1/3 cup snipped chives, fresh
- 2 tbsp. lime juice, fresh
- 2 tbsp. lime zest, grated

For latkes

- 2 lbs. sweet potatoes
- Salt, kosher
- 1/2 cup onion, chopped finely
- 3 beaten eggs, large
- 1/3 cup flour, all-purpose
- 2 tsp. chili powder, ground
- 2 tsp. cumin, ground
- 1 tsp. baking powder, reduced sodium
- 1/2 tsp. cinnamon, ground

To deep fry: oil, sunflower or canola

For garnishing: chopped cilantro, fresh, if desired

Instructions:

1. Prepare sour cream lime sauce. Stir sour cream, lime juice, zest and chives together in small sized bowl. Allow flavors to develop as you're making latkes.

2. Shred sweet potatoes with med./fine shredding disc on your food processor. Transfer them to colander and sprinkle with 1/2 tsp. of kosher salt, +/-. Squeeze out excess moisture with your hands.

3. Put shredded sweet potatoes in large sized bowl. Add eggs, onion and flour. Salt as desired. Add cinnamon, baking powder, cumin and chili powder. Mix till combined well.

4. In heavy skillet or deep fryer, heat oil on high till hot, but not till it smokes. Fill 1/4 cup measuring cup with the latke batter. Drop into your other hand and squeeze out excess liquid. Slip latke into heated oil. Flatten latke with spatula. Continue to make the latkes in this way, cooking four or five at one time.

5. Fry latkes till crisp and golden on bottom, four minutes or so. Turn carefully and cook other sides. Continue till all batter is used. Transfer cooked latkes to layered paper towels for draining.

6. Serve latkes promptly, with sauce and garnish as desired.

17 – Deep Fryer Spring Rolls

Visitors to the Bahamas may have already tried these deep-fried spring rolls. You can easily make them at home, and they're a great appetizer for friends and guests.

Makes 2 Dozen Rolls

Cooking + Prep Time: 1 1/2 hour

Ingredients:

- 3 cups of coleslaw mix (7 oz. or so)
- 3 chopped green onions
- 1 tbsp. of soy sauce, low sodium
- 1 tsp. of oil, sesame
- 1 lb. of chicken breasts, skinless, boneless
- 1 tsp. of salt, seasoned
- 2 x 8-oz. pkgs. of softened cream cheese, light
- 2 tbsp. of chili sauce, Sriracha
- 1 x 24-28 count pkg. of wrappers, spring roll, frozen thawed

To deep fry: oil, vegetable

Optional: chili sauce, sweet

Instructions:

1. Toss the onions, coleslaw mix, sesame oil and soy sauce. Allow to stand while you fry the chicken.

2. Bring four cups of filtered water to boil in medium pan. Reduce the heat and maintain simmer. Add the chicken and cover. Cook till internal temperature is 165F, about 15 to 20 minutes. Remove the chicken and cool it slightly. Chop the chicken finely and toss with the seasoned salt.

3. Mix chili sauce and cream cheese in large-sized bowl. Stir in the coleslaw mixture and the chicken.

4. Place 2 tbsp. of filling below middle of wrapper with a corner facing you. Fold the bottom corner over that filling. Moisten other edges using water. Fold side corners in towards the middle, over the filling. Roll tightly and press to seal. Repeat with remaining wrappers and filling.

5. Heat the oil to 375F in deep fryer or electric skillet. Fry the spring rolls, several at once, till they are golden brown, turning occasionally, six to eight minutes per batch. Drain them on layered paper towels. Serve with the chili sauce, if desired.

18 – Deep Fried Perfect Fries

These deep-fried, homemade French fries are as delicious and crispy as you'll get at your favorite fast food restaurants. Plus, they have none of those mysterious ingredients that fast food restaurants use.

Makes 4 Servings

Cooking + Prep Time: 1 hour 20 minutes

Ingredients:

- 2 lbs. of peeled, sliced 1/4" x 1/4" russet potatoes – after you cut them into sticks, keep them submerged in water in a bowl
- 2 tbsp. of vinegar, white, distilled
- Salt, kosher
- 2 quarts of oil, peanut

Instructions:

1. Pour vinegar in pan and add potatoes. Add two quarts of filtered water plus 2 tbsp. of kosher salt. Bring to boil on high. Boil for 8-10 minutes. You want tender potatoes, but you don't want them falling apart.

2. Drain potatoes. Spread on rimmed cookie sheet lined with paper towels. Allow them to dry for five minutes or so.

3. Heat the oil to 400F in deep fryer or large wok. Add 1/3 of the fries to the oil. Temperature of oil will drop down to about 360F. Cook for 45-50 seconds and agitate occasionally using wire mesh strainer. Remove to second rimmed cookie sheet lined with paper towels. Repeat with remainder of potatoes in two additional batches. Allow the oil to heat back up to 400F after each batch. Serve promptly.

19 – Deep Fryer Lime Chili Chicken Wings

Who could have known that a mixture of lime juice, maple syrup, and chili sauce could make deep-fried chicken wings so great? Be sure to make plenty, because family and friends won't be able to keep their hands off these chicken wings.

Makes 2 Dozen Wings

Cooking + Prep Time: 1 hour 20 minutes

Ingredients:

- 2 1/2 lbs. of chicken wings, whole
- 1 cup of syrup, maple
- 2/3 cup of sauce, chili
- 2 tbsp. of lime juice, fresh
- 2 tbsp. of mustard, Dijon
- 1 cup of flour, all-purpose
- 2 tsp. of salt, kosher
- 2 tsp. of paprika, sweet
- 1/4 tsp. of pepper, ground

To deep fry: oil, canola

Optional: lime wedges thin-sliced green onions

Instructions:

1. Slice the wings in three sections and discard the tips. In large pan, combine syrup, lime juice, mustard and chili sauce. Bring to boil. Cook till liquid reduces to one cup or so.

2. Combine flour, paprika, kosher salt ground pepper in wide, shallow dish. Add the wings, several at once. Coat by tossing.

3. In deep fryer or electric skillet, heat the oil to 375F. Fry several wings at a time for six to eight minutes, till they have no pink to them anymore. Use paper towels to drain wings.

4. Transfer the wings to large sized bowl. Then add the sauce mixture. Toss and coat well. Serve promptly, with lime wedges and green onion slices, if desired.

20 – Deep Fried Cauliflower

This is a favorite snack for game days, regardless of the sport that you're watching. The battered cauliflower is cooked ultra-crispy and tossed in a garlicky, wonderful buffalo sauce.

Makes 4-6 Servings

Cooking + Prep Time: 20 minutes

Ingredients:

- 2 quarts of oil, peanut or vegetable
- 1/2 cup of corn starch
- 1/2 cup of flour, all-purpose
- 1/2 tsp. of baking powder, reduced sodium
- Salt, kosher
- 1/2 cup of water, cold
- 1/2 cup of vodka
- 1 x 1"-floret-cut cauliflower head
- 1/3 cup of sauce, hot, like Frank's
- 1 minced garlic clove, medium

Optional: 1/4 cup of celery leaves, pickled

Instructions:

1. Preheat the oil to 350F in deep fryer or large sized wok.

2. Combine corn starch, baking powder, flour 2 tsp. of salt in large-sized bowl. Whisk till you have a uniform consistency. Add vodka and water. Whisk till you have formed a smooth batter. Add extra water bit by bit if you need it. The consistency should be like thin paint.

3. Add the cauliflower to thin batter. Work with one wing piece at a time. Lift one. Allow the excess batter to drip away. Lower piece carefully into heated oil. Repeat with remaining pieces of cauliflower till fryer is full. Don't overcrowd.

4. Fry and use a metal strainer to agitate and rotate pieces so they will cook evenly. They should be crisp and golden brown all over, six minutes or so. Transfer pieces to plate lined with paper towels. Season promptly with kosher salt. Keep first batch warm while you cook the last batch.

5. Combine the hot sauce, minced garlic plus 1 tbsp. of oil from the deep fryer in large-sized bowl. Whisk and combine well. Toss cauliflower with the sauce. Sprinkle with the celery leaves, if you like, and serve promptly.

21 – Deep Fryer Jalapeno Poppers

If you're a barbeque fan, these jalapeno poppers will be one of your favorite appetizers to make – and eat. You can also stuff the peppers using cooked beef or chicken.

Makes 6 Servings

Cooking + Prep Time: 1 hour 10 minutes

Ingredients:

- 6 jalapeno peppers, large

To deep-fry: oil, vegetable or canola

- 1 cup of shredded, BBQed, cooked pork, refrigerated
- 1 cup of cheddar cheese shreds, mild
- 1/4 cup of BBQ sauce
- 1 cup of flour, all-purpose
- 1 cup of corn starch
- 3 tsp. of salt, kosher
- 3 tsp. of paprika, sweet
- 12 oz. of beer or non-alcoholic beer

Optional: BBQ sauce, white

Instructions:

1. Slice and remove stems from ends of jalapeno peppers. Remove the seeds and the membrane.

2. Bring eight cups filtered water to boil in large pan. Add the jalapenos. Leave pan uncovered and cook only till the peppers are crisp but tender, two to three minutes. Remove peppers. Drop into a bowl of water and ice. Drain. Pat till fully dry.

3. In deep fryer or electric skillet, heat the oil to 375F. Mix the BBQ sauce, cheese and pork in small sized bowl. Spoon this mixture into the jalapeno peppers. In separate bowl, whisk the corn starch, flour, paprika and salt. Stir in the beer till barely moistened.

4. Use tongs to dip the stuffed jalapeno peppers into the batter. Fry them in batches till they are golden brown, three to four minutes. Drain them on layers of paper towels. Serve with white BBQ sauce, if desired.

22 - Deep Fried Pork Chops

These thin and tasty pork chops will be coated in a bread crumb, sage, and Parmesan cheese mixture. Then they're deep-fried till wonderfully crispy outside and juicy and tender inside.

Makes 4-6 Servings

Cooking + Prep Time: 25 minutes

Ingredients:

- 8 x 1/2"-thick pork chops, center-cut
- Salt, kosher
- Pepper, ground
- 1 cup of flour, all-purpose
- 4 beaten eggs, large
- 2 cups of breadcrumbs, panko, crushed
- 1 oz. of Parmigiano-Reggiano cheese, grated
- 1 tbsp. of minced sage leaves, fresh

To deep fry: 1 – 1 1/2 cups of oil, canola or vegetable

Instructions:

1. Season the pork over its entirety using kosher salt ground pepper. Set three shallow wide bowls on your work surface.

2. To the first bowl, add flour. To the second, add the beaten eggs. To the third bowl, add Parmesan cheese, sage and breadcrumbs. Season Parmesan panko as desired. Mix well.

3. Start with one pork chop. Dredge it in flour and shake off any excess. Transfer it to the egg dish and coat both sides. Lift and allow any excess egg to easily drain off. Transfer pork chop to breadcrumb mixture. Scoop breadcrumbs on pork and press gently, making sure to cover both sides. Then transfer the pork chop to a clean cookie sheet lined with baking paper. Repeat with remainder of pork chops.

4. Fill deep fryer or large, deep skillet with 1/4" of oil. Heat on high till oil shimmers but does not smoke.

5. Using your fingers or tongs, lower chops gently into hot oil, laying them away from you so they won't splash in your direction. You can work in batches, as desired. Fry while rotating chops so they brown evenly. They should become crisp and browned. Flip the pork chops. Fry until opposite sides are also crisp and browned. Transfer to layers of paper towels for draining. Lightly salt. Repeat steps with remainder of chops and serve.

23 – Deep Fryer Sweet Potato Chicken Bites

Do you want to spice up your chicken bites? Try this recipe. The sweet potato chips add flavor and crunchy texture and the meat stays nice, and tender inside.

Makes 4 Servings

Cooking + Prep Time: 35 minutes

Ingredients:

To deep fry: oil, canola or vegetable

- 1 cup of sweet potatoes, sliced thinly into chips
- 1/4 cup of flour, all-purpose
- 1 tsp. of salt, kosher
- 1/2 tsp. of pepper, ground
- 1/4 tsp. of baking powder, sodium-free
- 1 tbsp. of corn starch
- 1 lb. of 1"-cubed chicken tenderloins

Instructions:

1. In deep fryer or electric skillet, heat the oil to 350F. Place the flour, chips, 1/2 tsp. of kosher salt, ground pepper baking powder in food processor and pulse till ground well. Transfer to shallow, wide dish.

2. Mix remainder of salt with corn starch. Toss with the chicken pieces. Toss with the sweet potato chip mixture and gently press to coat.

3. Fry the chicken bites, several at once, till they are golden brown, two to three minutes. Drain them on layered paper towels. Serve.

24 – Deep Fried Chicken Livers

The chicken livers in this deep fryer recipe are a bit sweet, with a creamy, rich texture. Those sweet notes in alcohol pair well with their subtle sweetness.

Makes 4-6 Servings

Cooking + Prep Time: 1 hour 20 minutes + 1 hour marinating time

Ingredients:

- 1 lb. of chicken livers
- 1 tbsp. of sauce, hot, + extra to serve
- 3/4 cup of buttermilk, low-fat
- 1/2 cup of flour, all-purpose
- 2 beaten eggs, large
- 1 1/2 cups of breadcrumbs, panko
- 1 quart of oil, peanut, vegetable or canola
- Salt, kosher

Instructions:

1. Trim away fat and connective tissue from chicken livers. Cut livers into halves. Combine 1 tbsp. hot sauce and the buttermilk in medium-sized bowl. Add chicken livers. Marinate chicken livers in refrigerator for an hour or longer.

2. Drain chicken livers in sieve. Place eggs, breadcrumbs and flour in three separate wide, shallow bowls. Dredge livers in flour first, then in egg, then in breadcrumbs. Place breaded livers on rimmed cookie sheet.

3. Pour 1" oil in deep fryer or heavy skillet. Heat oil on med-high till it has reached 350F. Place the breaded livers in hot oil in batches. Fry them, occasionally turning, till crisp and golden, three to four minutes each side. Transfer livers to paper towel-lined platter. Use salt to season. Serve chicken livers with extra hot sauce on the side.

25 - Deep Fryer Mac Cheese Nuggets

This dish was created for a lover of mac and cheese. It is even more delicious than the original, because of its deep-fried, crispy outside coating, and its creamy richness inside.

Makes 20 Appetizers

Cooking + Prep Time: 1 hour

Ingredients:

- 2 cups of pasta shells, small, uncooked
- 20 pasta shells, jumbo, uncooked
- 2 tbsp. of butter, unsalted
- 1 x 16-oz. pkg. of cubed Velveeta processed cheese
- 2 cups of cheddar cheese shreds
- 1 cup of whipping cream, heavy
- 3/4 cup of Parmesan cheese, grated
- 1 1/4 cups of milk, 2%
- 2 eggs, large
- 2 cups of breadcrumbs, panko
- 1/2 cup of flour, all-purpose

To deep fry: oil, canola or vegetable

Instructions:

1. Cook the large and small pasta shells in separate pans, using instructions on package. Drain well. In large sized pan, melt butter on low. Add 1/4 cup of Parmesan cheese, cream, cheddar cheese and Velveeta cubes. Cook while stirring on low heat till blended well. Remove pan from the heat.

2. In separate large pan, combine smaller pasta shells 1/2 cheese mixture. Set it aside. To make the dipping sauce, add and stir 1 cup of milk into the remainder of the cheese mixture. Keep it warm.

3. In another shallow, wide bowl, whisk the eggs and remainder of milk. In a separate shallow, wide bowl, mix remainder of Parmesan cheese with breadcrumbs. In third bowl, place the flour.

4. Fill large pasta shells with a bit less than 1/4 cup of pasta mixture. Dip the shells in flour, coating all sides. Shake excess off. Dip large shells in egg mixture, then in the breadcrumb mixture. Pat to help the coating to adhere to shells.

5. Heat the oil to 375F in deep fryer or electric skillet. Fry the shells, several at a time, for one to two minutes per side, till a dark golden brown. Then drain the shells on layered paper towels and serve them with the dipping sauce.

Deep frying gives desserts a new look and a new taste. Try some of these favorites soon...

26 – Deep Fried Blueberry Sugar Egg Rolls

These blueberry egg rolls have awesome taste, and they're easy to make. They are just pie filling in the egg roll wrappers, deep-fried, then topped with powdered sugar, if you like. Yummy!

Makes Various # of Servings

Cooking + Prep Time: 25 minutes

Ingredients:

- Egg roll wrappers, large
- 1 can pie filling, blueberry
- 1 egg, large for the egg wash

For deep frying: oil, canola

Optional: powdered sugar

Optional: ice cream, vanilla

Instructions:

1. Heat two to three inches of oil in deep fryer or deep pot up to 350F.

2. Lay out wrappers and add about 2 tbsp. blueberry pie filling in middle of each. Don't overfill them.

3. Moisten edges with egg wash. Bring sides inward and then roll up.

4. Fry till they are golden on each side. Allow to cool. Dust with powdered sugar and serve. Add ice cream beside the egg rolls, if you like.

27 – Deep Fryer Churros

These churros only take several minutes to deep-fry, and they are still great tasting, even at room temperature. This **Makes** them a wonderful dessert for a party.

Makes 16 Servings

Cooking + Prep Time: 50 minutes

Ingredients:

For churros

- 1 cup of water, filtered
- 6 tbsp. of butter, unsalted
- 2 tbsp. of sugar, granulated
- 1 tsp. of vanilla extract, pure
- 1 cup of flour, all-purpose
- 1 tsp. of salt, kosher
- 2 eggs, large
- Sugar-cinnamon mixture

For dipping sauce

- 3/4 cup of chocolate chips, dark
- 3/4 cup of cream, heavy
- 1 tsp. of cinnamon, ground
- 1/4 tsp. of salt, kosher

Instructions:

1. In large-sized pan on med. heat, add the water, sugar and butter. Bring to boil. Add vanilla. Turn heat off. Add salt and flour. Stir till mixture thickens, about 30 seconds. Allow the mixture to cool for 8-10 minutes.

2. Use a hand mixer to beat eggs into the cooled mixture, one after another, till all is combined. Transfer the mixture to piping bag with large open tip.

3. In deep fryer or large-sized pot on med. heat, add oil enough to go halfway up sides. Heat to 375F. Hold piping bag several inches above oil. Pipe churros carefully into 6-inch ropes. Use scissors to cut dough off from the piping bag.

4. Fry churros till golden, four to five minutes, turning as needed. Fry a few at a time and allow the oil to raise back to 375F before starting a new batch. Remove churros and roll in sugar-cinnamon. Place on cooling rack.

5. Place the chocolate chips in med. heat-proof bowl. In small-sized pan on med. heat, bring cream to simmer. Pour the hot cream over chips. Allow them to set for two minutes. Add sugar-cinnamon and salt. Combine by whisking. Serve the churros with the chocolate flavored dipping sauce.

28 – Deep-Fried Cookie Dough, Oreo® Twinkie® Balls

In its base of cookie dough batter, you can add not just cookies and Twinkies, but any type of candy or sweet that you prefer. It's often made for county fairs, and it's not difficult to make at home.

Makes 20 Servings

Cooking + Prep Time: 25 minutes

Ingredients:

- Cookie dough
- Twinkies®
- Oreos®
- 1 cup of flour, all-purpose
- 2 tsp. of baking powder, low sodium
- 1/2 tsp. of salt, kosher
- 1 tbsp. of sugar, granulated
- 3/4 cup of milk, whole
- 1 beaten egg, large
- 2 tbsp. of unsalted butter, melted

Instructions:

1. Freeze the Twinkies and Oreos for two hours or longer. Overnight is great.

2. Heat oil to 375F.

3. Whisk other ingredients till smooth.

4. Bring out frozen treats several at a time.

5. Drench in batter. Shake off a bit.

6. Fry for 1 to 1 1/2 minutes per side

7. Top with powdered sugar. Serve warm.

29 – Deep Fryer Apple Fritters

Deep-frying apple fritters is easier than one think. The best apples to use for this dessert are Granny Smith since they hold up wonderfully when you fry them. You can use other kinds too, though, if you prefer.

Makes 20 Pieces

Cooking + Prep Time: 45 minutes

Ingredients:

- 4 apples, medium
- 2 cups of flour, all-purpose
- 1/2 cup + 2 tbsp. of sugar, granulated
- 2 eggs, large
- 2 cups of buttermilk, light

To deep fry: 2 cups + 4 tsp. oil, vegetable

- 3/4 tsp. of cinnamon, ground
- 2 tsp. of baking soda, reduced sodium
- 1/2 tsp. of salt, kosher
- 1/2 tsp. of sugar, granulated

Instructions:

1. Combine 1/2 cup of sugar with cinnamon in medium bowl. Set it aside. In separate bowl, whisk in 4 tsp. of oil, buttermilk and eggs. Gradually add sugar, baking powder, salt and flour.

2. Add 2 cups of oil to deep fryer. Heat to 375F. Slice apples. Coat with flour batter. Deep fry them. Flip when cooked on one side, so other side cooks. Fry till crisp and golden brown.

3. Transfer apples to paper towels. Toss sugar and cinnamon over them. Serve while hot.

30 – Deep Fried Funnel Cakes

These funnel cakes are always favorites at county fairs and festivals across the US. They can be topped with whipped cream and strawberries, or with powdered sugar, chocolate sauce, or fruit sauce.

Makes 20-30 Funnel Cakes

Cooking + Prep Time: 45 minutes

Ingredients:

- 3 beaten eggs, large
- 2 cups of milk, 2%
- 4 cups of flour, all-purpose
- 1/3 cup of sugar, granulated
- 1/2 tsp. of salt, kosher
- 1 tbsp. of baking powder, low sodium

To deep fry: 1 quart of oil

- 1/4 cup of sugar, sifted, powdered

Instructions:

1. Whisk milk and eggs in medium bowl.

2. Sift flour, baking powder, sugar and salt together. Add to milk eggs. Beat till smooth.

3. Heat oil in your deep fryer to 375F. Hold funnel and keep opening closed with a finger. Fill it with batter.

4. Hold funnel over heated oil. Remove your finger from funnel end. Allow batter to run out in stream into heated oil. Move the funnel from center and swirl outward.

5. Fry for two to three minutes, till golden brown. Transfer fried cakes to layered paper towels and drain. Shake the powdered sugar over funnel cakes. Serve.

Conclusion

This deep fryer cookbook has shown you…

How to use the different ingredients to affect unique fried tastes in dishes both well-known and rare.

How can you include deep frying in your home recipes?

You can…

- Make breakfast empanadas and deep-fried French toast, which you may not have heard of. They are just as tasty as you would imagine.
- Learn to cook with beer batter, which is sometimes used in deep frying. You can always use non-alcoholic beer if you prefer.
- Enjoy making deep-fried seafood dishes, including tilapia, catfish, and cod. Fish is a mainstay in most regions, and there are SO many ways to make it great.
- Make dishes using potatoes and cheese, which are often used in deep-frying.
- Make various types of desserts like deep-fried churros and funnel cakes, which will tempt your family's sweet tooth.

Have fun experimenting! Enjoy the results!

Author's Afterthoughts

Thanks ever so much to each of my cherished readers for investing the time to read this book!

I know you could have picked from many other books, but you chose this one. So, a big thanks for reading all the way to the end. If you enjoyed this book or received value from it, I'd like to ask you for a favor. Please take a few minutes to **post an honest and heartfelt review on *Amazon.com*.** Your support does make a difference and helps to benefit other people.

Thanks!

Julia Chiles

Printed in Great Britain
by Amazon